00459

SOUTHCOATES PRIMARY SCHOOL
SOUTHCOATES LANE
HULL
HU9 3TW

musical instruments
around the world

Godfrey Hall

Wayland

Titles in this series:
Clothes Around the World
Festivals Around the World
Food Around the World
Houses Around the World
Musical Instruments Around the World
Shops and Markets Around the World
Toys and Games Around the World
Transport Around the World

Cover pictures: Steel band, British Virgin Islands. Musician in Rajasthan, India. Violin and accordion players in Budapest, Hungary. Sousaphone player, USA.
Contents page: Conch shell being used as a musical instrument, Fiji.

Book editor: Alison Cooper
Series editor: Deb Elliott
Book design: Malcolm Walker
Cover design: Simon Balley

First published in 1995 by
Wayland (Publishers) Limited
61 Western Road, Hove
East Sussex BN3 1JD

© Copyright 1995 Wayland (Publishers) Limited

British Library Cataloguing in Publication Data
Hall, Godfrey
  Musical Instruments Around the World –
  (Around the World Series)
  I. Title II. Series
  784.19

ISBN 0 7502 1565 8

Typeset by Kudos Design Services
Printed and bound by Rotolito Lombarda s.p.a.

Thanks to the Royal College of Music, Sue Hall, and Toucan of Bond Street, Brighton.
Picture Acknowledgements
The publishers would like to thank the following for allowing their pictures to be reproduced in this book:
J Allan Cash 19 (top), 24; Eye Ubiquitous *contents page* (Eric Smith), 7 (top, Eric Smith; bottom, Thelma Sanders), 9 (top, Pam Smith), 13 (bottom, Julia Waterlow), 15 (Matthew McKee), 16, 20 (Paul Thompson), 29 (top, Nick Wiseman); Robert Harding 5 (top; bottom, Nigel Francis), 8, 11 (top, Christopher Rennie), 14 (top, Rob Whitrow), 26 (bottom); Redferns 10 (Odile Noel), 12 (David Redfern), 19 (bottom, Odile Noel), 21 (bottom, David Redfern); Rex Features 29 (bottom); Peter Sanders 9 (bottom); Tony Stone Worldwide *cover* (top left, Oliver Benn; top right, David Hanson; bottom left, Christopher Cole; bottom right, Doug Armand), 4 (Hilarie Kavanagh), 11 (bottom, Patrick Cocklin), 13 (top, Ben Edwards), 14 (bottom, Steve Climpson), 17 (top, Stephen Johnson; bottom, Christopher Cole), 18 (Bruno De Hoques), 21 (top, Peter Poulides), 25 (Oliver Benn), 26 (top, Oliver Benn), 27 (Oldrich Karasek), 28 (Tom Raymond); Wayland Picture Library 6, 22 (APM Studios), 23 (APM Studios).
Commissioned photographs arranged by Zoë Hargreaves.

Contents

Making music............................4
Something simple.....................6
Flutes and pipes.......................8
Sitars and guitars 10
Bows and strings 12
Big and beautiful 14
A bit of brass 16
Banging the drum 18
All in one...............................20
Shake and rattle......................22
Bands.....................................24
Orchestras..............................26
Playing together......................28
Glossary 30
Books to read 30
More information....................31
Index 32

Making music

There are all sorts of different musical instruments around the world. Most are played by blowing, banging or plucking. This Gambian cora is played by plucking the strings with your thumbs.

People enjoy playing music on their own, with their family and friends, or as part of a group.

Music is very important on special occasions. This piper is playing bagpipes at a ceremony in Scotland.

Something simple

Many instruments can be made from simple materials. Try blowing across the top of an empty milk bottle to make a sound.

People in the Pacific Islands make holes in the sides or ends of conch shells and use them like trumpets.

In Africa and the Middle East the horns of rams and antelopes are used as musical instruments.

SOUTHCOATES PRIMARY SCHOOL
SOUTHCOATES LANE
HULL
HU9 3TW

Flutes and pipes

There are lots of instruments that are played by blowing. In Malaysia, there is a flute that is played by blowing down it with your nose!

Pan pipes are often used in South American music. Pipes of different lengths are stuck together to make the pan pipes, and each pipe makes a slightly different sound when you blow into it.

In India, snake charmers use an instrument called a pungi. This is made from a gourd and a cane. As the snake charmer plays, the snake rises out of its basket and sways to the music.

One of the simplest flutes in the world is called a nay. The players blow down one end of the flute to make the sounds. It can be very difficult to play.

Sitars and guitars

The sitar is an Indian instrument. It is played by plucking the strings. There are seven strings on the outside and between nine and thirteen strings on the inside.

These men in Peru are playing stringed instruments. The bigger one is a guitar and the smaller one is called a churrango.

Many pop groups use electric guitars. Electric guitars can make a louder sound than other guitars.

Bows and strings

Some stringed instruments are played using a bow. The bow is usually made out of horsehair and it is scraped across the strings to make the sound. Fiddles are played in this way, and they are found in many different countries.

The sarangi is an Indian instrument that is played with a bow.

This Chinese man is playing an erhu.

Big and beautiful

These are Alpine horns. They make deep sounds when you blow into them.

These men are playing Tibetan horns and large drums.

Didgeridoos come from Australia. A didgeridoo is usually made from a piece of wood that has been hollowed out inside by termites. It can be up to two metres long. You can see one being played in this band.

A bit of brass

The trumpet is popular in Central and South America. It is an important instrument in the southern part of the USA, where it is played in jazz bands.

Trumpets are also played in brass bands, along with other instruments such as trombones and tubas. This bandsman is playing a tuba.

The sousaphone is a kind of tuba, but it is bigger than an ordinary one. The 'tube' goes right round the player's body.

SOUTHCOATES PRIMARY SCHOOL
SOUTHCOATES LANE
HULL
HU9 3TW

Banging the drum

Drums are often used in African music. They are used in ceremonies and to beat out the rhythm when people are dancing. They can be made from wood or clay.

These drummers are taking part in a ceremony outside Buckingham Palace in London. Their drums have to be light enough for them to carry as they march.

The most spectacular instrument in an orchestra is the kettle drum. It is played with large beaters.

19

All in one

This Portuguese woman is playing an accordion. She presses the black and white keys on the keyboard at one end, and the buttons at the other. She also has to squeeze the middle section in and out, to make the sound.

Another instrument with keys is the piano. Many children start to learn the piano when they are very young. Pianos are used in orchestras and by some pop singers.

An organ player has several rows of keys to play, instead of just one, and he or she also has lots of foot pedals to press. When the keys are pressed, air is pushed through big pipes to make a sound.

Shake and rattle

Rattles and shakers can be made from dried gourds or tubes that have been filled with seeds or tiny stones. This South American shaker makes a sound like falling rain when it is tipped upside down.

These shakers are called maracas. They often contain dried seeds.

Bands

Bands are used in ceremonies and celebrations. This is a women's marching band in The Netherlands. They are taking part in a procession to celebrate their Queen's birthday.

Steel bands are very popular in the Caribbean and wherever West Indian people live around the world.

Orchestras

Up to one hundred people play in a symphony orchestra. A lot of different instruments make up the orchestra – violins, cellos, flutes, drums, trumpets and many others.

Not all orchestras use the same kinds of instrument. This orchestra in China uses traditional Chinese instruments.

This man is playing the violin at a concert in the Czech Republic. Famous orchestras travel all over the world to give concerts.

Playing together

Sometimes it's more fun to play with other musicians than on your own. These men are playing folk music together.

These Russians are playing in the street to earn money from people passing by. The big stringed instrument is a balalaika. It looks too big to carry around!

Many pop groups use electronic instruments and computers to make music.

29

Glossary

band A group of musicians. Some bands use just one type of instrument, such as brass instruments.
brass Brass instruments have to be blown to make a sound.
cello A large stringed instrument played with a bow.
ceremony An event that marks an important occasion.
electronic Powered by electricity.
flute An instrument made from a hollow tube of wood or metal. You blow into the mouth hole and cover the holes down the side with your fingers to change the sounds.
folk music Music that is passed on through the family.
gourd The fruit produced by some plants that belong to the cucumber family. Dried gourds can be used to make shakers.
jazz A type of music that began among black people in the southern USA about a hundred years ago.
orchestra A large group of musicians, usually playing lots of different types of instrument.
plucking Pulling or tugging the strings of a musical instrument.
termite A type of ant that lives in warm, tropical parts of the world. Some termites eat wood.
trombone A brass instrument. The player blows into a tube and slides a part in and out to change the sound.

Books to read

Live Music series (*Brass, Keyboards, Percussion, Strings, The Voice, Woodwind*) by Elizabeth Sharma (Wayland, 1992)
The Music Funshop by Sebba (Evans, 1993)
Musicians by David Marshall (Macdonald Young Books, 1993)
Sound and Music (*Starting Science* series) by Kay Davies and Wendy Oldfield (Wayland, 1991)

More information

Would you like to know more about the people and places you have seen in the photographs in this book? If so, read on.

pages 4–5
The Gambian cora is made from a gourd which has been cut in half, hollowed out and covered with animal skin. It has twenty-one strings.
Jazz band playing in the French quarter of New Orleans, USA, a city famous for jazz music.
Bagpipes are usually associated with Scotland, but different types of bagpipes are also played in Northumberland in England, in Ireland and in some parts of Europe. The bags were once made from the skin of a whole sheep or goat, but are now made of leather, rubber, or artificial materials.

pages 6–7
Man blowing conch shell in Fiji.
A sacred tribal horn, Ghana.

pages 8–9
Playing pan pipes in Ecuador. Pan pipes can be made up of between three and fifty pipes stuck together.
A snake charmer entertaining tourists in Bombay, India.
Playing nay flutes on Lamu Island, Kenya, in celebrations to mark the prophet Muhammad's birthday.

pages 10–11
The sitar comes from northern India. A wire plectrum is used to pluck the strings.
The guitar was probably first developed in Spain in the early sixteenth century. The churrango is a South American form of the guitar and parts of it are made from an armadillo's shell.
The electric guitar was invented in 1928. Its sound is amplified electronically. Modern pop groups usually have a lead guitar and a bass guitar.

pages 12–13
The fiddle was first developed in Europe in the tenth century and may have been based on an Arab instrument, the rabab.
Sarangi player in Jaisalmer, India. The man beside him is playing a harmonium, a keyboard instrument.
The erhu is the Chinese version of a violin. This blind busker is playing in Sichuan, China.

pages 14–15
Horn players taking part in an alp horn and yodelling competition in Switzerland. Alp horns were originally made so that people could signal to one another from the tops of the mountains.
Monks playing Tibetan instruments at the Thikse Monastery in Ladakh, India.
Didgeridoos are a traditional instrument of the Aboriginal people of north-east Australia.

pages 16–17
Trumpet player busking in Battery Park, New York, USA.
Trumpet-like instruments have been in use for thousands of years – a silver trumpet was found in the tomb of the ancient Egyptian king Tutankhamun.

Tubas similar to those in use today were developed in Germany in the first half of the nineteenth century. Many brass bands in England were formed by factory and mine owners in the nineteenth century for their workers.
The sousaphone is a twentieth-century invention, named after J P Sousa, a US composer and bandmaster. As it is worn round the body, it is easier to carry while marching.

pages 18–19
Traditional Ninga drummers in the central African state of Burundi.
The pipe and drum band of the Coldstream Guards leaving Buckingham Palace.
Kettle drums probably developed in the Middle East over a thousand years ago, possibly as pot drums formed by fastening a skin over a clay pot. They are usually played in pairs, and can be carried by horses, elephants or camels in parades. Orchestral kettle drums are usually known as timpani.

pages 20–21
The accordion is a European instrument; the piano accordion (the type shown here) was developed in the mid-nineteenth century in France and Italy.
The piano was invented in Italy in the first part of the eighteenth century.
A type of organ was played by the ancient Greeks; the Egyptians and Romans used similar instruments.

pages 22–3
These shakers are known as rain-makers or water-pipes. They come fron Ecuador and are made from bamboo or the stems of cactus plants.
Maracas are traditionally made from dried gourds. They are often used in Spanish and Latin American music.

pages 24–5
Marching band in a procession in Marken, in The Netherlands, to mark Queen Beatrix's birthday.
Steel band playing at an Easter festival in the British Virgin Islands.

pages 26–7
The Royal Philharmonic Orchestra in London. String, brass and woodwind instruments can be seen, as well as the large kettle drums at the back.
Chinese orchestra performing in Beijing.
Violinist playing in the Dvorak Hall, Prague, in the Czech Republic.

pages 28–9
Folk group playing in a house porch in Tennessee, USA.
Street musicians busking in Leningrad, Russia. The balalaika is a traditional Russian instrument; it is usually triangular, with three strings.
The-pop group The Pet Shop Boys using electronic equipment in their performance.

Index

accordion 20
Africa 4, 7, 18
Alpine horns 14
Australia 15

bagpipes 5
balalaika 29
bands 15, 24
  brass 17
  jazz 16
  marching 24
  steel 25

Caribbean 25
Central America 16
China 13, 26
churrango 11
conch shells 7
cora 4
Czech Republic 27

didgeridoos 15
drums 14, 18-19, 26
  kettle 19

electronic instruments 29
erhu 13

fiddles 12
flutes 8-9, 26
folk music 28

Gambia 4
guitars 11

horns
  Alpine 14
  animal 7
  Tibetan 14

India 9, 10, 13

Malaysia 8
maracas 23
Middle East 7

nay (flute) 9
Netherlands, The 24

orchestra 19, 21, 26-7
organ 21

Pacific Islands 7
pan pipes 8
Peru 11
piano 21
pop groups 11, 21, 29
Portugal 20
pungi 9

rattles 22
Russia 29

sarangi 13
Scotland 5
shakers 22-3
sitar 10
sousaphone 17
South America 8, 11, 16, 22

Tibet 14
trumpets 7, 16, 17, 26
tubas 17

USA 16

violin 26, 27

32

SOUTHCOATES PRIMARY SCHOOL
SOUTHCOATES LANE
HULL

SOUTHCOATES PRIMARY SCHOOL
SOUTHCOATES LANE
HULL
HU9 3TW